He Chose Me

CHERLYN GRESHAM

HOV
PUBLISHING

HE CHOSE ME

Copyright © 2022 by Cherlyn Gresham

HOV Publishing a division of HOV, LLC.
www.hovpub.com
hopeofvision@gmail.com

Contact the author Cherlyn Gresham
Email: cherlynsix@gmail.com

Cover Design: Hope of Vision Designs

Editors: HOV Publishing

For more information about special discounts for bulk purchases, please contact Cherlyn Gresham or HOV Publishing

ISBN: 978-1-955107-70-9

10 9 8 7 6 5 4 3 2 1

Printed in the United States of America

DEDICATION

I dedicate this book first and foremost to God. Without the change made from within me, this book could not be possible.

iv

ACKNOWLEDGEMENTS

I would like to thank my stepmother, Joan Logan, had it not been for her over these years, encouraging me to put my life on paper, I wouldn't have the courage to write this book.

Then to my sisters, Uannah Carpenter and Antoinette Chavis, life has not always been so easy for us. It is only through the grace of God, the gift and talent of words; that a portion of our story

can be written. We are survivors!

SPECIAL THANKS

A special thanks to Tenaria Drummond- Smith and HOV Publishing for giving me a voice for the chosen. I will be forever grateful for the opportunity given to me and so many other powerful women of God. You give a voice to the silent. You give a voice to the hurt; you give a voice to those bruised and misused but to God be the glory. We love you.

TABLE OF CONTENTS

CHILDHOOD YEARS

Growing up as little girl in the City of New York, there were many unanswered questions. Learning and becoming a woman was hard. My Mother was a functional coke addict who abused her children by leaving them alone to raise each other. My sisters and I had to become Survivors.

I do not know that I can say I learned what being a woman was, I basically learned how to survive. I was raised by my mother, she had been married to my "Father" and from that marriage, came my oldest sister and me. Then she married my Stepfather and from that marriage came my youngest sister. It was at that time that we moved around a lot, never knowing where we would be next.

We stayed with friends of my mothers, until we were able to get a solid place of our own. My aunt would come and get me often during the weekends, she was a Jehovah Witness, now this was my great aunt Dot and she favored me, of all my sisters. I grew up in a weird family, I am sure no crazier than others.

My grandmother never wanted us around, I remember always going to her house hearing her say, yawl kids get away with all your barking (coughing) but ended up keeping us on occasion, my aunts favored my oldest sister, I guess because she was lighter than me and my youngest sister. No one really took to my youngest sister. I believe because they did not like my mother's decision when it came to my stepfather.

My mother was very abusive, and we girls were to be seen and not heard. We were to agree with anything she said, even if she were wrong, or we could expect to be beaten. This is an example starting from the age of 6 that I can remember and never forget.

My mother and stepfather were having a fight and living in a duplex apartment at that time; my stepdad asked us to go downstairs while him and my mother argued.

My mother of course did not agree, she stated that we were her three bitches, and we were to listen to her. So, she told us to sit down in birth order while we watched them fight. My mother told my stepdad to leave; he had an option walking out or being carried. So, my stepdad picked up the cast iron frying pan and hit my mother upside her head. Without a moment's notice my mother stabbed him in the gut. I guess he got carried out.

Next example happened around the same time where while my mother and stepdad were separated, my sisters and I became early snoops, or detectives. My mother worked and we had to be home either with a babysitter or on our own. I was only in the first grade. My sisters and I had come home and yes, like any other children, we were curious. We had gone into my stepdad's closets and found porno comics. We thought it was interesting… remember we were only 6 and 7 years old.

Now why we decided to take these magazines to school is beyond me, but with no judgement we did. It just so happened that this day was show and tell. LOL

While sitting in the class of course showing off the magazine at the worst possible time, the teacher asked me what I had to show that day. Now understand that we never have been able to bring anything to school because we were poor, and we did not have anything to show; Ever. So, this seemed to be a good idea at the time until the teacher came to the back of the class and looked at what I was showing the class. I got sent straight to the principal's office. I begged them not to call my mother because she was crazy, but no one ever listens to children.

Ok! We came home from school petrified, not knowing what my mother would think of next to do to us. After a while, my mother came home, and she told us to strip. So, all three of us frightened to death at what my mother would do, we took off our clothing down to our panties.

She had this stick called the nigger be good stick. This stick was about an arm length long round almost to resemble a police stick, wooden wrapped in black rubber, my soon to be stepdad made this instrument for my mother to beat us with it.

She got an extension cord and rope and tied my wrist together, then my ankles, and to top it off, she stuffed a folded pair of socks in my mouth to prevent me from screaming, this is what is called being hog tied. After this she preceded to beat us within an inch of our life as if we were slaves. The weps were so bad that our skin was cut and bleeding on our butt, legs and back.

The next day as if nothing happened, we went to school to live another day. We could not sit in our seats we were beaten so bad. Well with this came ACS, and more, but we were never taken from our mother; she was too smart for that. Now that was my childhood years and two examples of the abuse we suffered.

YOUNG TEEN YEARS

I am a young teen around thirteen years of age and by this time I had been abused by my mother, molested by my uncle and the maintenance guy, trying to talk to a mother that never listened never helped. I got into boys early in life because they were the only ones that seem to want me. I could be anything any man wanted me to be, and this seem to work for me, so I thought.

By the time I was thirteen, boys were the only thing on my mind because they noticed me, they listened to me, and they pretended to care. It did not matter that we went to the best schools, because most of the time we were alone hungry eating mayonnaise, ketchup, mustard sand-wiches, by this time my mother had moved to the borough where the rich stepdad lived, she finally gave him a son, so I guess her three little bitches went out the door.

To get to my mother's other house in the borough with my rich stepdad, I remember having to jump the train because I didn't have money to get a ticket so I could get food from their deep freezer. Our clothes were dirty, we washed everything by hand as we were taught because Mother was not giving us any money. I remember only one time she gave us $10 in total to wash our clothes.

I could not take it no more, if this was love, it was killing us. My sister tried to commit suicide, to get away from my mother. She eventually ended up leaving home to stay with my aunt and my youngest sister is the only one that actually ended up staying with my mother until her dying day. When I was 13 years old, I was dating this boy and I am guessing because she couldn't control the situation, she had me locked up, into a group home environment with girls I should have never been around.

Only my sisters understood being raised in this manner and without a father of my own, being an abused woman becomes second nature to you. Love should not hurt but it did for me. As a young woman growing up, I was screaming out for help to no avail. I was looking for love in all the wrong places but never knew what it was.

I wanted to come back home but that did not happen until three years later; after being in thirteen different group homes and one foster home with a Foster mother who worked. She kept me educated and dressed, but every Friday she would go to the bar with her female friend and come home coked up and drunk. She would pull me out of the bed and call me the devil; she said I was evil. That is funny, she almost sounds like my mother when she said I would never be shit. I would only be good enough to be a whore and my pussy was going to fall out.

So, between this and leaving school, it took thirteen blocks to walk down Corona

Avenue to get to the train to lay with the next guy I saw, and it was only three blocks to catch the school bus. Before I knew it… I had missed over 100 days of school. That is when the law was signed if you were 16, and nowhere near graduating they had the right to kick you out of school; and that is exactly what they did.

The One thing I always held on to from my mother's survival rules:

1. Never trust a man to do anything for you.

2. Always be independent.

3. If they offer you anything, that is fine and good but always be able to provide for yourself.

4. If you have a habit, do not depend on anyone else, only yourself.

So, she raised us to be independent strong black women, but she left a whole in our hearts, and we all have our story and this one is mine.

With this I ran to the first man that showed he loved me. *Statistics call it **"Daddy issues"** is an informal phrase for the psychological challenges resulting from an absent or abnormal relationship with one's **father**, often manifesting in a distrust of, or sexual desire for, men who act as **father** figures.* Go figure. They were all 10 to 11 years older than me. I never knew why.

YOUNG ADULTHOOD

By the time I was 18, I had literally become a chameleon. I was taught to adapt under any circumstance and that is what I did.

I had my first child; a daughter at the age of 18. I was married to my first husband by 19 and he made me abort my child at five months because it wasn't his child. I gave birth to my second child; a son when I was 20. My third child; a daughter was conceived through rape by my husband at 21. I divorced my first husband because of domestic violence. I married my second husband and had my fourth child; a son was born. Three years later I adopted my fifth Child, a daughter. I know I was crazy! But I had so much love to give.

I remember wanting kids so bad. I wanted a family that loved me, so since I never received it, I was going to create it. I have always been full of life and love with no one to share it with because they all had an agenda of not loving me. I was cheated on and I still married my first husband at the age of 19 thinking I was in love or that someone loved me. He beat me basically every other day for two years. He had isolated me from family and friends, but the ultimate abuse, was when my first husband raped me. Oh, I forgot it's not rape if it's your husband...The devil is a Liar. My third child; a daughter was the blessing God had given me. I had so many babies, but he wanted to keep me barefoot and pregnant so no one else would want me.

I could not take it no more I left him after the fateful decision to kill myself, but then I thought where my kids would go; then I thought about him and said never!

I had to get away from that situation so, I strategically with the help of his mother planned my getaway at 8 months pregnant with my third child.

I was now about 21 years old married to my abuser, living in a domestic violence shelter. One day I decided I was not going to keep this child because of how it came about. So, I ventured out with my double stroller and my babies in it and on my way to the abortion clinic.

While walking down the street and tears in my eyes, I heard a voice say "Stop, turn around you're not going to do this". I looked and there was no one around me, I continued to walk; Then it came again..."

Stop, turn around! "She belongs to Me!" What was this, I couldn't fathom.

It was the voice of the Lord! He told me that she belonged to Him, and I was going to return her to Him, then he said "Look up this is her name" the Lord had Stopped me Infront of Trinity Baptist Church.

It was then that I started my journey with the Lord and learning How to become a woman of God. This would be the moment that would truly shift all things in my life. Now I did not say everything was suddenly alright; in fact, it was about to get harder. So, for the first time like a fish out of water, I took on a life of faith; I stepped out and leaned on Jesus.

This baby was number three, and her name was going to be Trinity. As I said before, I was in a battered women's shelter and I ended up going back to my husband for a while. The sentimental me, was going to get me killed. If you have ever been close to my situation, then you know how hard it is to venture out on your own at 21 years old with two children 3 years old and under and one on the way. We seem to think we cannot make it; or at least this was what we are brainwashed to believe. God was with me, and he took me through all my wrong decisions, as He has been since the beginning. I had gotten to the point of suicide at 8 months pregnant. When I made up in my mind that enough is enough, while in my PJ's, I left in the middle of the night with three babies, and one of them was not mine, but I was not about to leave anyone behind.

The next twenty years brought the marriage of my second husband and two more children and a change in my life. I fell into those same mistakes with drugs, being with a man that did not know how to love me, and I never loved him. He was safe, he was not going to hit me, he seemed to be a man of God, and he did not hang out in the street. Oh! and he did not mind raising my children with me. There was just one problem, we were unequally yoked, and when I was advised not to Marry him, I disobeyed God: not my pastor.

That disobedience brought twelve years of division in my home. Years of disrespect, dysfunctional for sure; but whose is not. Eventually a separation that was inevitable. I spent twelve years in a marriage and was not faithful once. Well after this, I did something that I do not usually do; I took a two-year sabbatical to reflect on me, my wants, my needs, my desires, and my dreams. I spent so many years chameleonizing myself to fit everyone else, I did not know who I was.

I continued through all of this, to go to church, knowing and feeling that there was more for me. I never gave up, but I was tired, and it was going to take this last experience to turn my life around forever.

I met someone on the way to church one day, this person was going to be the one

God used to open my eyes for real. I fell so hard it was not funny and as usual I was in love. I was really wondering at this point whether I knew what love was. I spent the next eight years learning the hard way, that God was always the only love I needed.

It is now September 2018, and my life was now at the lowest it could possibly be. I had started smoking crack, through this so-called love, who did not love me, but used my goodness that I never knew was there. I had become severely stricken in my body to where I was almost a vegetable for five years. I've had two strokes, a heart attack and five ungrateful children who could not see their mother had disappeared right before their eyes.

The depression had gotten so bad, I did not want to be here anymore. Why was this so hard? Why was this my life? Why did all those I love, hate me? I say that because love does not hurt, love is not jealous, insecure, but its patient and kind. Between all the relationships with men, my marriages to abusive men, an abusive mother, and to top it off; my own children, fighting with them and them being abusive as well; I was done. I felt if I had been cursed, being so rebellious, not being obedient, bedding many, and faithful to none; this I thought was my fate.

But God! One day I just fell to my knees after a huge argument with one of my daughters and in the corner of my room is where I was going to end it all. But instead, I turned to where I had been running from my whole life, God. I cried and pleaded with the Lord, to save me, I did not want to live like this anymore. I did not want to hurt or be hurt anymore. Always looking to be validated by others while sinking further into sin. I decided the only validation I needed, was knowing I was a child of the King. Then it was almost instantaneous while at a service at church, I received the Holy Ghost once again. I had been renewed, forgiven, and set free. Now it was up to me.

ADULTHOOD

I went into 2019 with the thought, "For God I live and for God I Die". Forgetting those kids and men, and just concentrating on the Lord and my walk with Him. It was only the first week in the year 2019, and I found out by my overseer, that I was being honored. I said for what? Living? She said your living for God, right? It was done. My ceremony was to take place July 29, 2019. I need you to pay close attention, this is going to be quick but filling. Do not miss it.

In February I went out and received a gift shape like a pillowcase. I had only $8 to my name. I took a cab to return home and when I arrived at my destination, I opened my bag to money flying all around the cab, I felt like I had just robbed a bank. Where did this money come from? Scared to death, I heard a voice say, you owe no man nothing.

This was strange because I had received a letter saying that I owed rent, but I did not owe anything. I was going to get this business straight and little did I know, it was already taken care of for me.

I rushed home where my nephew was sitting, and I told him immediately to pay off whatever debt I had. Then in March, I took a friend of mine to a school where I volunteer and do missionary work. It was there that the next few words I heard would change my life forever. The voice said it's time now to start the church. Many years prior, my Bishop had told me it was time to start my church, but I paid her no mine when I left the church. I knew what I was doing, and I was nowhere near starting a church of my own. These words came to me again after almost 10 years later. So, then I was told to buy the laptop. Now a little tidbit about that. Five years prior I had asked the Lord why I had been punished and why did I get all that education in Law and graduating salutatorian of my class in business if my life were to become this. I also asked, why was I in the church caught up in all the gossip and backbiting, and one day I saw the devil on the pulpit. Why was I in this situation? I never got an answer.

Well, I am sitting at the computer, and I am doing what God told me; to listen and follow. I began typing and before I knew it, I had an entire PowerPoint presentation on the ministry including the mission statement. I was amazed and wondered where this came from, I then heard that voice again say "Now do you know why I gave you that education? Now can you see? I put you in that church to show you yourself, what you had become, and now that you have truly received deliverance and your spirit is grieved, you are now ready to receive what I had to give. I put you in the world to receive the education that would later be used for my Glory; but I had to pull you out and lay you down because the world was pulling you from me.

I was in tears. The next few months was spent building the ministry. July had come and it was now time for my honoree ceremony. I had been honored and ordained as Minister. I kept hearing in my spirit, "you will not be here past the summer". Time was quickly flying by until one day in August, I received a call from Arizona saying that the home I applied for two years prior was ready. I had been walking by faith and not by sight, so I got on the plane August 31st, 2019, and other than packing up and turning in my old key to the landlord, I told myself that I will never return to that city.

It is now January 2021 and in one year and a few months I have become a Pastor/ Overseer, with Women in Christ Ministries being born in March and now we have been in operation for nine months. I worked on a book project, and it became an Amazon #1 bestseller. I became a #1 bestselling author. I got a job with the state of Arizona and a beautiful car. I also received my license to operate my business in both Arizona and Florida, where I just come back from during a pandemic to ordain two of my ministers.

To top it off, in the beginning of 2020, I received a vision of a man in my dream. I never knew this man. I started attending church and one day this man from my dream walked into the church. Where did he come from? Why was he in my dream? I even pulled him to the side and asked him who he was and why was he in my dream. As you can imagine, he looked at me like I was crazy and said, "well I don't know miss, why was I in your dream"? we both laughed; and before you knew it, we had become the best of friends. Me being alone in a new state, he became very convenient. I did not have a car at that time, and I was still being restored so I was using a walker. He was extremely useful. I was able to depend on him, our friendship grew stronger and stronger. He had an issue where he had to be delivered and I was delivered looking for a change, that could only take place with God. Who would have known wed both be delivered unto one another.

A year has passed, and we became truly fond of each other. I had never known a love quite like this. We are both believers of Christ and are equally yoked. Especially important, God gave me my heart's desire through obedience, a partner in life, and a partner in Christ. Someone who would love me for me. Someone I could trust, and he trusted me. Someone who I could say completed me. How is it that I was so blessed, when at one time I was stressed and depressed? I was finally able to let my guard down because I knew God finally had me. For Christmas we became engaged! WONT HE DO IT???

Now you want to know what it feels like to be a woman. I would have to say it is the hardest thing ever. With all the confusion, disrespect, childhood issues that drive you into a world of chaos; we as women go through the fire just to come out as gold. Our test and trials come to build us and make us strong. This is what God did for me, he turned me into a proverbs 31 woman (Virtuous).

So, with me taking in the bad and the good, but looking unto God through it all, being a woman has been a wonderful journey, but becoming an anointed woman of God, is better.

ABOUT THE AUTHOR

To begin, I was born a Catholic, but raised as a Jehovah's witness. I got saved in a Pentecostal church and now I attend Higher Dimension Christian Center. My mother taught me how to live and survive in the world and my aunt Dorothy taught me the way of Jehovah. It was then that I was introduced to God. My aunt Dorothy used to make me recite Psalms 83:18 over and over again, but I still didn't know him.

The first time I heard the Lord's voice I was on my way to an abortion clinic with my third child. He said "Turn around you're not going to do it. I kept on walking. He said it again. The third time he said she belongs to me, and you will return her to me. Then he said look up this is her name; the Lord had stopped me in front of Trinity Baptist Church.

It wasn't until I had my fourth child I was truly introduced to God. I received salvation while attending Lively Stone Pentecostal Church.

> *⁵ Trust in the LORD with all thine heart; and lean not unto thine own understanding.*
>
> *⁶ In all thy ways acknowledge him, and he shall direct thy paths.*
> Proverbs 3:5-6 (KJV)

That would become my favorite scripture because it was with that trust and faith, I started to serve God. Also, being abused and used, I was taught to live in fear, but 2 Timothy 1:7 says *For God hath not given us the spirit of fear; but of power, and of love, and of a sound mind.*

I Graduated salutatorian in law and business, and I minored in English where God Helped me to develop my gift of writing. I became an educator of disadvantage youth, being proactive in my community. Teaching Entrepreneurship and raising six children. My house has always been a House of refuge where, I have always taken in children that God has given me with issues that needed prayer and needed the Lord.

During the last twenty years, I have been an Usher, Sunday School teacher, financial secretary, and I served in the kitchen for the church. I have led Sunday morning devotional service, I sung on the choir and I directed the children and adult choirs. I still love singing for the Lord. I was ordained Missionary Evangelist and now God has blessed me to become a shepherd leader of Women in Christ Ministries.

God chose me. He chose me at a time in my life where I was at my worst, and He still loved me. Not knowing that I was called, for many are called but few are chosen. I, like so many others have endured trials, tribulations, and hardships, but I see now that who I am and all that I've been through was to prepare me for such a time as this.

The message that the Lord gave me was to go after his women and bring them back to Him. I use my story to give God glory because He loved me when I didn't love myself and all the things done in my past was never meant to last. I praise and thank God for the vision of the ministry that is in three different states now, in Florida, North Carolina, and Arizona where we use technology to give God glory.

My prayer for this book is that women all over will be able to identify with my story, and to know the God has called them. This has been a mission that I have accepted and so with my story I'm giving God glory that I may bring His women back to Him as He has chosen me to do. Becoming a shepherd leader is not an easy task but it's the most elite and humbling task that a servant can be given in my opinion.

It really isn't about where you come from but it's where you end up. I started out a young girl in New York City living a life that was given to me without God. Now I live in Arizona with my wonderful husband Jesse Gresham, that I have been truly blessed with, and a life of prosperity and abundance that I could have never imagined I would ever have, had God not been on my side.

This book is just a sample of what is to come, and I pray that it's a great read for every one of you out there. I'm not asking that you just read this book I'm asking that you read this book meditate on this book and ask God what about this book that you should take for your life. Without God we are nothing. If He can choose me, He can and will choose you.

From Amazon Bestselling
Co-Author

Cherlyn Gresham

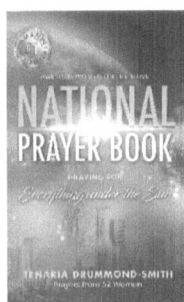

Available at

www.ingramcontent.com/pod-product-compliance
Lightning Source LLC
Chambersburg PA
CBHW031254120626
46545CB00007B/2801

* 9 7 8 1 9 5 5 1 0 7 7 0 9 *